WILDE'S
LEISURE GUIDES

Cycle route guide to 50 leisure trails in Norfolk, Suffolk & Essex

WRITTEN BY GILLIAN ROWAN-WILDE

Published by

GILDERSLEVE
PUBLISHING LIMITED

GENERAL INFORMATION

Wilde's Leisure Guides are a trade mark of Gildersleve Publishing Ltd.

© Copyright Gillian Rowan-Wilde

Published by
Gildersleve Publishing Ltd
Capricorn House, Blackburn Road
Rising Bridge, Lancashire BB5 2AA

ACKNOWLEDGMENTS
To the Access and Public Rights of Way Officers in Norfolk, Suffolk and Essex, also The Broads Authority for their help and advice in their specific areas.

Last but not least the originators of all the trails without which it would have been impossible to start this journey.

Maps based upon Ordnance Survey mapping with the permission of the Controller of Her Majesty's Stationery Office,
© *Crown copyright 84393M*

THE OFF-ROAD CYCLING CODE

STAY ON THE TRAIL
Only ride bridleways & byways
Avoid footpaths
Plan your route in advance

GIVE WAY TO HORSES & WALKERS
Make sure you are heard when riding up behind anyone
Ride Carefully, keep to the left of anyone approaching you

NEVER RIDE IN LARGE GROUPS
5 or 6 is maximum

BE KIND TO BIRDS, ANIMALS & PLANTS
Keep your dog under control

PREVENT EROSION
Avoid skidding and locking your wheels when braking

CLOSE GATES BEHIND YOU
Don't climb walls or force hedges

EQUIPMENT FOR SAFETY
Wear a helmet
Take a first aid kit
Carry enough food and drink
Pack waterproofs & warm clothes
Take essential spares & tools

TAKE PRIDE IN YOUR BIKE
Maintain your bike before you leave, and on your return

BE TIDY
Take all your litter home
Never create a fire hazard

ENJOY YOUR CYCLING
Try not to get annoyed with anyone, it never solves a problem
Don't make unnecessary noise

RIGHTS OF WAY

Off-road cyclists have right of way on most public bridleways and other tracks unless forbidden by a bye-law. You must give way to walkers and horseriders.

By-ways, which are usually unsurfaced tracks are open to cyclists, as well as walkers and horseriders, you may also find vehicles have right to access.

There is NO right of way on Public Footpaths, if cyclists finds themselves on a public footpath they must get off their bike and walk.

A cyclist is NOT permitted to ride his bike on the pavements.

On moorland, upland or farmland a cyclist normally has NO right of access without the express permission of the landowner.

Tow-paths by the canals normally require a permit from the appropriate British Waterways.

There are quite a few designated cycle routes and paths to be found in urban areas, on Waterways tow-paths, Forestry Commission land or on disused railway lines.

Cyclists must adhere to the Highway Code.

GENERAL SAFETY HINTS

1. Make sure your bike is safe to ride before leaving home. It is advisable to take with you a puncture repair kit, a spare inner tube, and the necessary spanners and levers to help with your repair.
Don't forget your pump!
2. You must by law display working lights after dark.
3. Always carry some form of identification.
4. Always tell someone where you are going.
5. Learn the basic principles of first aid and take a small first aid kit.
6. Wear reflective material on your clothes, better to be seen.
7. Ride under control when going down hill, accidents can happen.
8. It is advisable to always wear a helmet.
9. Carry a water bottle, always keep it filled especially on a hot day. Take spare food, drink and clothing with you.
10. Be very careful when riding on marsh land or scree especially when it is wet.
11. Always take a detailed map with you for adventurous or wilderness trips. Have a compass with you. Take a whistle with you to use when calling for help should you have an accident.
12. Always be aware of others using the same path as yourself. They also want to enjoy their day out!
13. General maintenance of your bike on your return home. Making sure it is cleaned and oiled ready for your next trip.

ABOUT THE AUTHOR

Gillian Rowan-Wilde took up leisure cycling in the summer of 1993, her first trail being the Tarka Trail which she undertook during a holiday in Devon. To date she has ridden over 200 trails in compiling these guide books.

In this series of guides she hopes to bring to the leisure cyclist a catalogue of historical and interesting features on rides, together with some of the wildlife you may encounter.

MAPS BY

Andy Thelwell has grown up with Apple Macs and computer graphics. At present he is employed as a technical manager with a leading north west art studio

In his spare time he is either in the gym, or out off-road on his mountain bike.

ILLUSTRATION BY

Graham Nicholson studied illustration at Lincoln, since then he has been commissioned by many leading national, and international companies, supplying work for packaging, advertising campaigns and corporate brochures.

In his leisure time he is a keen walker, an interest he shares with his family.

INTRODUCTION

We were attracted to cycling in East Anglia after attending a seminar hosted by The East of England Tourist Board entitled 'Englands Cycling Country' held in Thetford in 1997 - of course being born and bred in Lancashire I did not believe that Norfolk, Suffolk and Essex were really Englands cycling country, especially having ridden and mapped over recent years the majority of the nations National Parks and recreational areas.

We were however to realise that this flat and undulating easterly bit of the UK, where earlier in its history the Roman invaders built great towns and roads, and the last great invaders the friendly American GI's left it with a legacy of disused airfields (which I might add can be great to cycle across) was to be a real surprise.

During the two years we spent compiling and riding the trails in this book we discovered that although the terrain was reasonably flat it certainly was not boring.

You can ride the forests of Thetford or Epping and many more, visit picturesque thatched villages, travel the old medieval routes, ride in the grounds of stately homes, tour the countryside by bridleway and byway or just meander along the old disused railways.

The length of routes in this book vary between 6 to 20 miles and the majority are graded easy to moderate, though very wet weather can make some trail sections difficult, these are marked in the relevant route descriptions.

Some bridleways, particularly those that pass through farm land, can vary in width and difficulty depending on how much the farmer leaves after ploughing his field!

Today more and more land is being set aside and opened up for recreational cycling - let us not abuse this initiative.

Please ensure when riding these routes that you comply with the Countryside Cycling Code (see page no 2). Please keep to the routes indicated and complying to any signage to the contrary as concessions may change.

As with our previous books we have included a list of cycle hire centres for people that need to hire - so get those legs going and enjoy the cycling that these three great counties have to offer.

Peter Gildersleve

KEY

i	Information Centre
P	Parking
WC	Public Convenience
☎	Telephone
⩍	Picnic Area
✠	Windmill
⚙	Cycle Hire
✝	Church
	Built up Area
	Quarry
—	Cycle Trail
....	Other routes/Bridleways
▬▬	Main Road
——	Minor Road
....	Footpath
•••●•••	Railway Track
⌒	River/Stream
	Marsh
◖	Lake/Reservoir
🌲	Mixed Wood
🌲	Coniferous Wood

CONTENTS

TRAIL GRADING

All trails have the O.S. map nos. given for guidance, so that the areas can be easily identified.

EASY
Old railway tracks. Towpaths on canals/rivers
No hills

EASY, ADVENTUROUS
As above but with a hill - easily negotiable

MODERATE
Forest paths Lakeside Moorland
A hill, Stream or rough ground - easily negotiable.

MODERATE, ADVENTUROUS
As above but possibly more than one hill - easily negotiable

HARD
Fells or forests with hills
Several hills with a degree of difficulty and ground may be undulating

HARD, ADVENTUROUS
As above but with steeper hills and steeper gradients

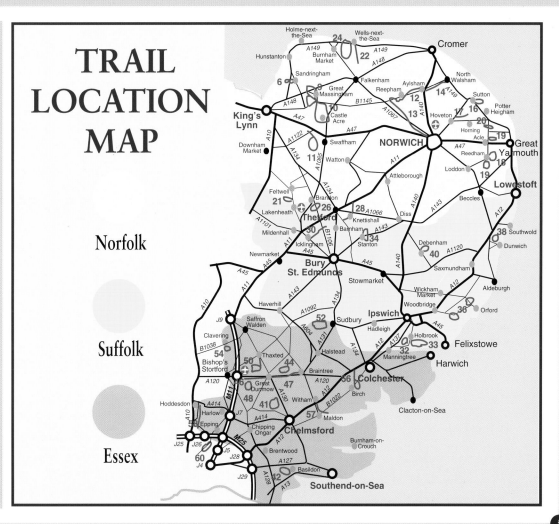

TRAIL LOCATION MAP

Norfolk

Suffolk

Essex

SANDRINGHAM COUNTRY PARK

START & FINISH: Visitor Centre Sandringham Country Park [S]

MAP: O.S. Landranger 132 N.W.Norfolk & King's Lynn

LENGTH: (approx) 10km (6 ¼m) Circular

SURFACE: Metalled/forest track

RIDE RATING: Easy

NOTES: *Beware - the A149 is a busy road take care crossing over and cycling along it.*

Sandringham is situated east of the A149, Kings Lynn to Hunstanton Road and west of the B1440. To the south is the A148 to Norwich.

This trail is a mixture of country lanes to Wolferton and forest tracks through the country park of Sandringham.

From the Visitor Centre turn left onto a wide track through the woodland and eventually coming out on the road beside a house called The Folly, turn right, carefully crossing the A149 and following the road into Wolferton. The old railway which had operated since 1847 used to stop at the station here to allow royal parties to alight before being taken to Sandringham.

Sandringham was bought in 1862 by Queen Victoria for her son Bertie, the future King Edward VII.
The beautifully laid out gardens and water landscapes as we see them today follow the traditions of great landscape designers such as Capability Brown.

Once back in the park, before returning to the centre, make time to visit the little church which is attended by the royal family when they are in residence. The gilded roof and the magnificent silver alter and pulpit front is something not to be missed.

Sandringham country park.

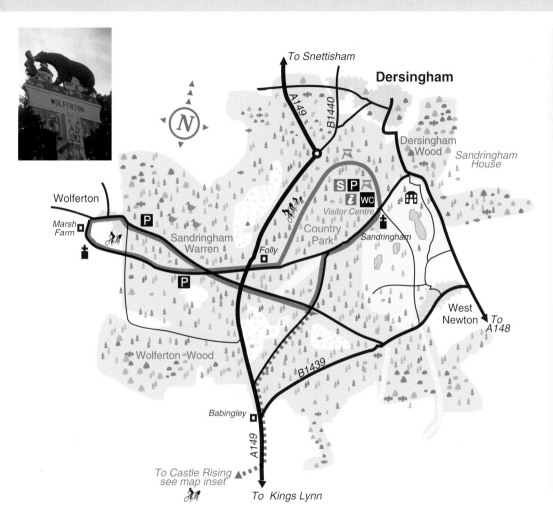

To Snettisham

Dersingham

A149

B1440

Dersingham
Wood

*Sandringham
House*

N

Wolferton

Marsh
Farm

P

Sandringham
Warren

P

P

Folly

Country
Park

S P
i WC

Visitor Centre

Sandringham

West
Newton

*To
A148*

B1439

Wolferton Wood

Babingley

A149

To Castle Rising
see map inset

To Kings Lynn

Castle Rising.

Babingley

*Whalley
Farm*

CASTLE
RISING

Hospital

i P
WC

CASTLE RISING

Approximate length of the route
from the Visitor Centre, Sandringham
to Castle Rising is 6km (3 ¾m)

This 12th century Norman Castle has
a wonderfully restored keep set in the
centre of massif earthworks, and is
well worth a detour.

PEDDARS WAY

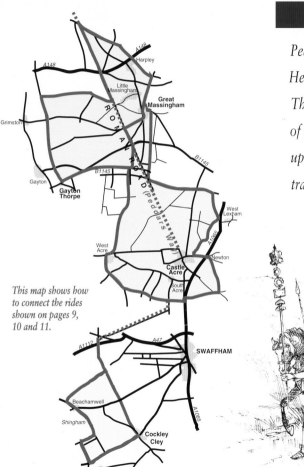

This map shows how to connect the rides shown on pages 9, 10 and 11.

Peddars Way is an ancient mainly Roman road running from Knettishall Heath near Thetford to Holme-next-the-Sea on the north Norfolk Coast. This 'road' was built with all probability after the defeat of the rebellion of the Iceni led by Boudicca in AD61 and originally ran from Colchester up to Lincolnshire with a ferry over the Wash. The surviving part of this track is 47 miles long and was officially opened as a recreational path in 1986 by HRH Prince Charles.

The countryside around this long straight stretch of Peddars Way is remote but has a harsh beauty. It is an area of outstanding natural beauty with a wide variety of birds and wild life living around the criss cross of ancient tracks over this heathland.

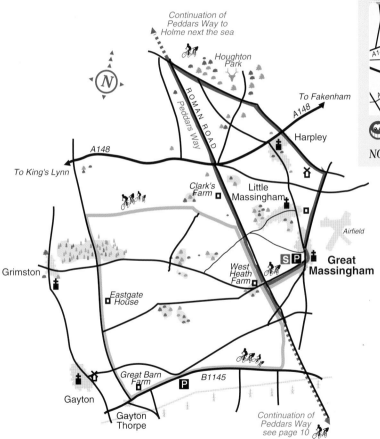

Continuation of Peddars Way to Holme next the sea

Houghton Park

N

ROMAN ROAD
Peddars Way

To Fakenham
A148

Harpley

A148

To King's Lynn

Clark's Farm

Little Massingham

Airfield

Grimston

West Heath Farm

Great Massingham

S P

Eastgate House

Great Barn Farm

P

B1145

Gayton

Gayton Thorpe

Continuation of Peddars Way see page 10

PEDDARS WAY *GREAT MASSINGHAM*

Market
Falkenham
Sandringham
Great Massingham
A148
B1145
A47
Castle Acre
A1122
A47
Swaffham

START & FINISH: Red/Brown Great Massingham S

MAP: O.S. Landranger 132 N.W.Norfolk & King's Lynn

LENGTH: (approx) Red 17km (10m) Circular Brown 22km (13 1/4m) Circular

SURFACE: Metalled/gravel/forest tracks

RIDE RATING: Easy Adventurous (both routes)

NOTES: This northern half of the Peddars Way is hard going after a rainy spell.

This section of the Peddars Way is situated north of the A47 and south and west of the B1153 and King's Lynn. To the east is the town of Fakenham.

The red route from Great Massingham via Peddars Way up to Houghton Park is a mixture of quiet lanes and a stoney track which is inclined to be very muddy after it has been raining. Houghton Hall within the Park was built by Sir Robert Walpole, first Prime Minister of England and the parkland around the mansion is well worth a detour before your return to Great Massingham.

The brown route from Great Massingham is a combination of bridleways and quite lanes. The heathland offers a superb ride through conifer plantations which are home to large colonies of Grey Squirrels and open countryside with wonderful views of the valley towards Great Bircham. There are a couple of lanes in the centre of the trail should you want to cut short your ride.

PEDDARS WAY *CASTLE ACRE*

START & FINISH: Great Massingham Village Green [S]

MAP: O.S. Landranger 132 N.W. Norfolk

LENGTH: (approx) 30km (18 ¾) Circular

SURFACE: Metalled/gravel

RIDE RATING: Moderate

NOTE: The unmetalled sections tend to get muddy after a severe downpour.

This section lies to the south of Great Massingham with the A47 to the west and the A1065 to the east. To the south lies the town of Swaffham.

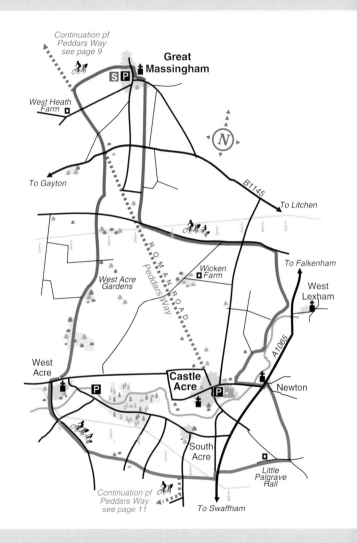

Continuation pf Peddars Way see page 9

Great Massingham

West Heath Farm

To Gayton

B1145

To Litchen

To Falkenham

West Lexham

Wicken Farm

West Acre Gardens

R O M A N   R O A D   Peddars Way

West Acre

Castle Acre

Newton

South Acre

Little Palgrave Hall

Continuation pf Peddars Way see page 11

To Swaffham

From Great Massingham pass to the left of the village pond and at the T junction turn left towards the mast. After a quarter of a mile turn left onto a concrete track and at the T junction with Peddars Way turn left.

Care should be taken after crossing the B1145 as you may miss the turning to your right off the Way onto a minor lane which will eventually take you down to the village of West Acre. Down the valley of the River Nar there are ruins of a large priory founded by the Augustinians, where today, the 14th century gatehouse is the only part still standing.

Castle Acre situated on the Peddars Way once boasted a huge Norman castle which was been built by Earl Warren, son-in-law of William the Conqueror, extending over 18 acres. Earl Warren also built the Priory south of Castle Acre for the Cluniac Order which was eventually swept away by the Dissolution, but today the beautiful west front of the priory church still stands.

The minor lanes and bridleways take you around in a southerly ark around Castle Acre up to Newton. The villages are a delight as you pass through them on your return to Great Massingham.

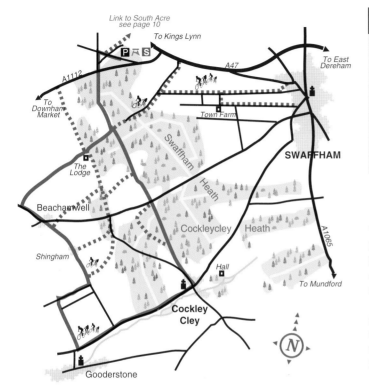

PEDDARS WAY *SWAFFHAM HEATH*

START & FINISH: Car park on the A1112

MAP: O.S. Landranger 143 Ely 144 Thetford & Diss

LENGTH: (approx) 21km (13m) Circular

SURFACE: Metalled/forest tracks

RIDE RATING: Easy adventurous

This trail is situated south of the A122 and north of the A134. Swaffham is to the north east, with the A1065 on the easterly edge of the route.

This trail is the cyclists detour of the Peddars Way, keeping to the west of Swaffham (the footpath section of the Way goes to the east of the town).

From the car park turn right on to the track through the forest (away from the A1112) until a crossing of tracks, turn left and over the very busy A1112 into Swaffham Heath.

The tracks through the woodlands are very pleasant with an abundance of wild flowers and birds, and a canopy of branches keeping you cool on a warm day.

At the southerly point of the Heath lies the village of Cockley Cley where there is the site of an Iceni Village, which is definitely worth visiting.

11

MARRIOTT'S WAY *AYLSHAM - REEPHAM*

START: Alysham - Bure Valley Railway Station [S]

FINISH: Reepham Station (on the trail)

MAP: O.S. Landranger 133 N.E.Norfolk

LENGTH: (approx)   11km(6¾m) Linear

SURFACE: Stone base/grit

RIDE RATING: Easy

This section of Marriott's Way from Aylsham to Reepham is situated north of Norwich. To the west is the A1067 with the A140 to the east.

The beginning of this trail is at Bure Valley Railway Station in Aylsham. The first half mile of the disused railway line is a rough track - (alternatively go via the road for this section but be vigilant crossing the main road from the railway station, turn right then left onto the B1145, under the bridge turn right and left onto Marriott's Way).

Aylsham is an old established market town where, in days gone by, the Wherries would have sailed up the River Bure to offlift their cargoes beside the mills in the centre of the town.

The trail uses the trackbed of the old Great Eastern Railway and the Midland & Great Northern line. Prior to 1948 the M&GM remained independent where the GER had become part of the Eastern Region of B.R. Two railway stations were built in Aylsham to accommodate both lines. During the second world war the railways were used quite extensively for both passengers and freight, and continued in use until their closure in 1959.

From Aylsham to Reepham Station the track has an excellent surface and is a very pleasant route for all cyclists. The trees and shrubs along the embankment give a little protection from the weather both rain and sun! the wild flowers are in abundance all along this well preserved route.

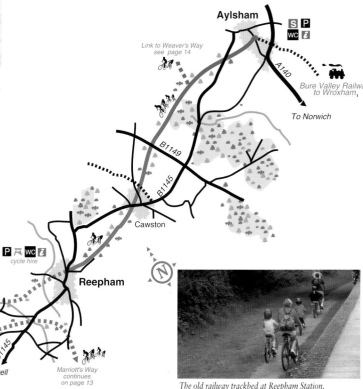

The old railway trackbed at Reepham Station.

Marriott's Way continues on page 13

START: Reepham Station off the B1145 `S`

FINISH: Marlpit Lane Car Park, off the A47

MAP: O.S. Landranger 133 N.E. Norfolk

LENGTH: (approx)   25km (15 ½m) Linear

SURFACE: Stone base/grit/grass

RIDE RATING: Easy adventurous

The route is situated north west of Norwich and the A1067, and east of the B1149. To the south is the River Wensum.

As an extension to this linear route - Using the railway line from Norwich, there is the facility of putting your cycle on the train to Wroxham, where you can pick up the narrow gauge Bure Valley Railway to Aylsham - making a circular route.

This trail is part of Marriott's Way, one of the longest recreational railway path in the country, 25 miles from Aylsham to the centre of Norwich.
The section from Reepham to Norwich is a rougher and narrower track than the first half of the Marriott's Way and if the weather has been inclement it may be very muddy. But nevertheless it is a very pleasant ride down to the City of Norwich along the old railway track bed. As the route is not as cultivated there are a wonderful variety of wild flowers, and the view of the surrounding countryside is excellent.

Soon after crossing the River Wensum for the third time you will reach the car park off the A47 this signifies the end of Marriott's Way - but you can continue on this traffic-free route the NCN (National Cycle Network) for a further 5 miles into the centre of Norwich.

Norwich Cathedral.

Continuation of Marriott's Way see page 12

Reepham

Themelthorpe

To Bawdeswell

B1145

Whitwell Hall

To Foxley

A1067

Lenwade

Attlebridge

Thorpe Marriot

Taverham

River Wensum

Drayton

NORWICH

A1067

A47

Marlpit Lane

Riverside Cycle Path to Norwich Centre (5 miles)

Aylsham

Reepham

North Walsham

A1067

A140

Hoveton

A47

NORWICH

A11

WEAVERS' WAY *NORTH WALSHAM - AYLSHAM*

START: North Walsham

FINISH: Aylsham - Bure Valley Railway Station

MAP: O.S. Landranger 133 N.E.Norfolk

LENGTH: (approx) 10km (6 ¼m) Linear

SURFACE: Stone base grit/metalled/grass

RIDE RATING: Easy adventurous

NOTES: *There is a bridleway through the grounds of Blickling Hall, west of Aylsham - route as shown on the map.*

The Weavers' Way trail is situated north of Norwich, between the towns of Aylsham and North Walsham in north east Norfolk. To the west is Blickling Hall and the A140 and to the east is the A149 and the coast.

Weavers' Way in its entirety is a long distance path of 92 km between Cromer and Great Yarmouth. The Way was named after the weaving industry which was introduced to Norfolk by Flemish Immigrants around the 12th century. North Walsham was an important centre for this industry.

The section between Aylsham and North Walsham lies along the route of the disused railway line that was once part of The Midland and Great Northern Railway between King's Lynn to Great Yarmouth. The railway line was closed in 1959, and now makes a wonderfully pleasant trail lined with shrubs and many varieties of wildflowers. Along the route the embankment is high enough to afford excellent panoramic views of the surrounding countryside.

BLICKLING HALL was built in the early 17th century and with its Dutch gables and dominant clock tower it is one of the most impressive Jacobean houses in England. The Hall is now owned by the National Trust and is well worth the detour.

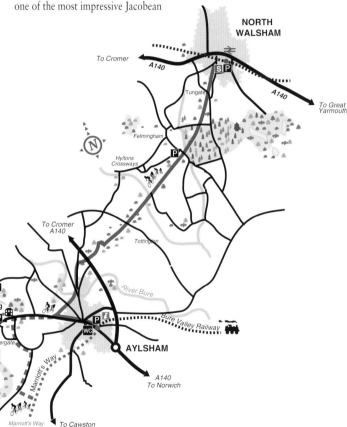

THE BROADS

The Broads are situated in Norfolk with the city of Norwich to the west. To the east are the towns of Caister-on-Sea, Great Yarmouth and Lowestoft.

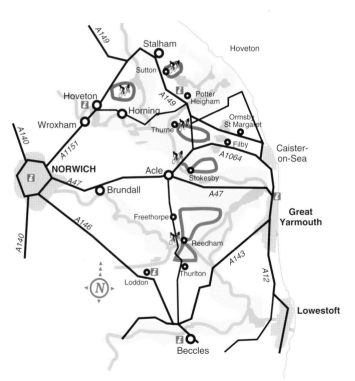

The Broads were formed by peat-diggers, the holes left by these diggers filled in with water producing shallow lakes which, over the years, created the Broads.

These routes within the Norfolk Broads are mainly along minor roads, there are no hills but gentle inclines, through beautiful countryside and pretty villages with views across the rivers, marshes and broadlands.

At the beginning of each of the routes there is the opportunity of hiring bicycles (some cycle hire centres are seasonal) and along the trails there are plenty of cafes and pubs where you can 'wet-your-whistle' (don't be 'over the alcohol limit' on your bike!) energy restored - enjoy the windmills, ancient churches and watching some of the restored Wherries with their great red sails moving gracefully over the waterways.

Boat Hire *For information on all boat hire on the Broads contact The Broads Authority Tel: 01603 610734*

THE BROADS *SUTTON - HICKLING BROAD*

START & FINISH: Sutton Staithe Boatyard (A149) S

MAP: O.S. Landranger 134 Norwich & The Broads

LENGTH: (approx) 14km (8 ³/₄m) Circular

SURFACE: Metalled

RIDE RATING: Easy

NOTES: *There are cycle hire points at both Sutton and Hickling Heath*

This route along the country lanes between Sutton and Hickling is very attractive with many buildings of interest, including the tallest windmill in the country - Sutton Mill with its milling machinery completely restored. and where you can view the broadland countryside from the top.

The village sign for Sutton depicts a Windmill and a trading Wherry - two of the best known images that conjure up 'The Broads'.

The Augustian Priory in Hicking is recorded in the Domesday Book of 1086, and is depicted on the village sign. The present priory dates from 1240 AD and contains many objects of ancient architectural value.

Hicking Broad, although very shallow is one of the largest - it is a nature reserve with reed beds sheltering Bearded Tits and Bitterns in season.

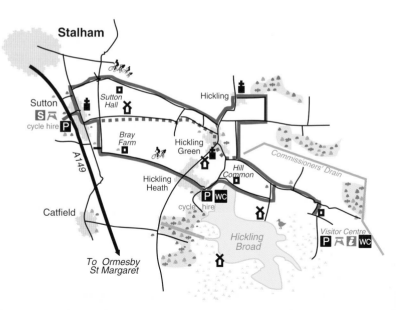

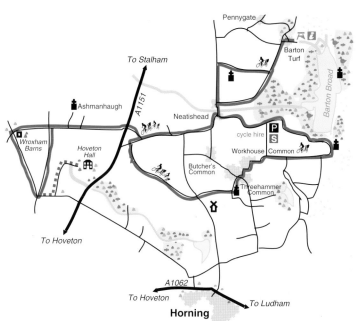

THE BROADS
WROXHAM BARNS - BARTON BROAD

START & FINISH: Car Park near Neatishead [S]
Barton Angler public house (Cycle Hire Centre)

MAP: O.S. Landranger 134 Norwich & The Broads

LENGTH: (approx) 19km (12m) Circular

SURFACE: Metalled

RIDE RATING: Easy

NOTES: This area of the Broads is very popular during the summer months please be aware of the extra traffic on the country lanes.

This route is on the country lanes to the north of Horning going past two famous churches, St. Michaels where some of the famous cricketing family Edrich are buried and St. Peter's, although rebuilt in 1970, has a font from the 14th century. The limes planted outside St Peter's Church are to commemorate local men who died in the Great War.

Go round the lanes to Hoveton Hall for a picnic in the designated areas in the woodlands or to the Wroxham Barns which have been converted from a collection of 18th century barns to workshops and rural crafts demonstrations, both are well worth a visit.

Barton Broad with all the water activities that surround this restored waterway is an ideal place to rest your weary legs and try a spot of sailing (see page 16 for boat hire information).

THE BROADS *HALVERGATE MARSHES*

START & FINISH: Reedham Quay

MAP: O.S. Landranger 134 Norwich & The Broads

LENGTH: (approx) 23km (9 ¼m) Circular

SURFACE: Metalled /stoney

RIDE RATING: Easy Adventurous

NOTE: Cross the railway lines north of Reedham with great care.

The town of Reedham (spelt 'Redaham' in the Domesday Book) lies on the bank of the River Yare, and was thought to be a Roman military garrison and later the seat of Edmund, King of East Angles (circa 855AD).

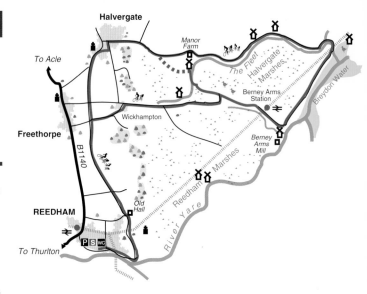

Commence this route from Reedham Quay, cycle towards the railway bridge that spans the River Yare and follow the road to the left up the hill. Turn right into Holly Farm Road and continue over the railway line. Take a left turn into Low Common and continue up the lane passing Reedham parish church of St John the Baptist on the right. Continue up the lane to the town of Halvergate.

In Halvergate turn right to join the track marked 'Weavers Way' across the Marsh. To take a short-cut follow the bridleway (red dotted line) to Berney Arms Station. These marshes are the largest expanse of marshland in Europe and rich in wetland wildlife - especially important for the birds during the winter months.

At Berney Arms Mill turn right past the Station taking the bridleway and track to Wickhampton and back to Reedham.

THE BROADS *REEDHAM - THURLTON*

START & FINISH: Reedham Quay

MAP: O.S. Landranger 134 Norwich & The Broads

LENGTH: (approx) 16km (10m) Circular

SURFACE: Metalled

RIDE RATING: Easy

NOTES: There is a charge for cyclists on Reedham Ferry

From Reedham Quay, beside the River Yare, turn left on to the B1140. The chain ferry over the River is the last remaining vehicle ferry on the Broads.

The splendid views over the River Chet and the reedbeds near Heckingham make this a very pleasant route. Heckingham church has a Saxon thatched round tower church with a wonderfully carved stone archway.

The Thurlton village sign depicts the All Saints church with its thatched roof and the 'Great Goliath' mill which was once the tallest in the area.

Once through the village of Thurlton there is a wonderful mixture of wooden barns and thatched houses to see before re-crossing the River Yare on your return to Reedham.

START & FINISH: Acle Bridge, alongside the River Bure [S]

MAP: O.S. Landranger 134 Norwich & The Broads

LENGTH: (approx) 17km (10 ½m) Circular

SURFACE: Metalled

RIDE RATING: Easy

NOTES: *Take care on these lanes as there will be other traffic visiting Thrigby Hall Wildlife Gardens (well worth a visit).*

This area used to be called Flegg Isle because in Roman times it was an island. Many village names end in 'by' indicating Danish settlements in 800-900 AD.

The start of this trail is in the car park on the A1064 opposite The Bridge Inn. Turn left out of the car park - be careful crossing this 'A' road as it can be very busy - continue along the lane to Stokesby. The Ferry Inn in Stokesby is where, until 1910, there was a ferry.

From Thrigby, across the River Bure should you want to shorten your route take the little lane south to Runham, rather than going round via Mautby.

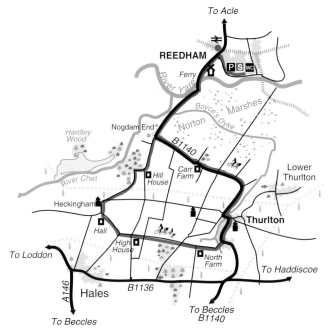

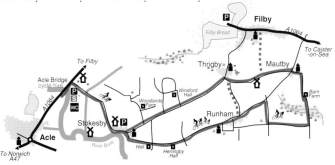

THE BROADS *THURNE*

START & FINISH: Thurne Village car park **S**

MAP: O.S. Landranger 134 Norwich & The Broads

LENGTH: (approx) 12km (7 ½m) Circular

SURFACE: Metalled/stoney

RIDE RATING: Easy

NOTES: *Take care when crossing the B1502*

The start of this route is in the car park opposite Thurne Dyke Mill in the village of Thurne. The name 'Thurne' is supposedly named after a great Danish Warrior, who may have lived in the Danish settlements in this area during the years 800-900 AD.

Turn right out of the car park and follow the lane till you reach a 'T' junction at this point cross the road on to the bridleway to the B1152 - at the cross roads cycle straight ahead and carry on round the lanes to

Burgh St Margaret. On your return, when you reach the B1152, should you want to extent your route turn left to Clippesby and back along the lanes (red dotted route). Otherwise continue straight over the B1152 back to

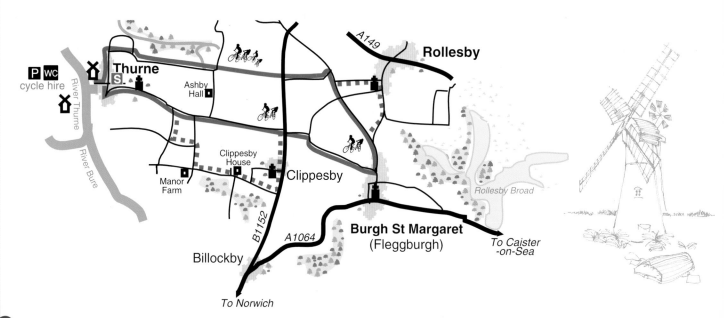

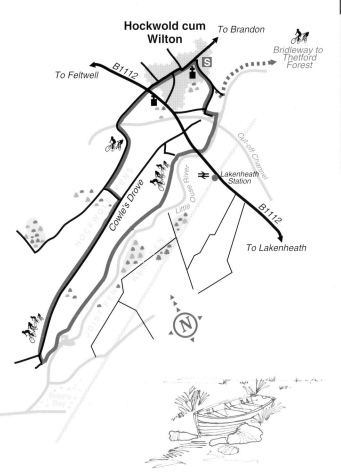

Hockwold cum Wilton

To Brandon

Bridleway to Thetford Forest

B1112

To Feltwell

Cut-off Channel

Cowle's Drove

HOCKWOLD FENS

JOIST FEN NEWFEN

Little Ouse River

Lakenheath Station

B1112

To Lakenheath

Botany Bay

N

HOCKWOLD CUM WILTON

Feltwell

Brandon

Lakenheath

Thetford

Mildenhall

market

Icklingham

A45

START & FINISH: Centre of Hockwold cum Wilton [S]

MAP: O.S. Landranger 143 Ely & Wisbech

LENGTH: (approx) 15km (9 ¼m) Circular

SURFACE: Grass/gravel

RIDE RATING: Easy

NOTES: *Take great care crossing the B1112*

This route following the banks of the Little River Ouse in Norfolk lies east of Thetford Forest and west of A1101. To the north is the small town of Feltwell and to the south is Lakenheath.

This route is on bridleways within the Fens west of the beautiful Forest of Thetford in Breckland.

The East Anglian Fens are a strange and beautiful place they are so open you can get quite disorientated, there are virtually no trees or hedges but open skies stretching over flat plains to the horizon.

The Hockwold cum Wilton route begins in the village and after crossing the B1112 follows the Sluice Drove over the Hockwold Fens to the junction and turns right on to Cowle's Drove.

As the track turns right keep left down to the path running along side the Little Ouse River. This is a very pleasant trail with excellent views across both New and Brandon Fens. On leaving the river continue along the cut-off channel before returning to Hockwold cum Wilton.

WELLS-NEXT-THE-SEA

START: Quay Car Park, Wells [S]

FINISH: Little Walsingham

MAP: O.S. Landranger 132 N.W. Norfolk & King's Lynn

LENGTH: (approx) 9km (5 ½m) Linear

SURFACE: Metalled

RIDE RATING: Easy

NOTE: *The Light Railway of Wells & Walsingham runs from Easter to end of September*

Wells-Next-The-Sea is on the A149 on the Northern coastline of Norfolk. To the west is Holkham Park and Burnham Market whilst to the east is Sheringham. The town of Fakenham is to the south.

Wells is a delightful fishing port with a lot of atmosphere. From the harbour you can watch the small fleet of whelk and shrimping boats as they return from a hard days work and unloading their catches.

There is a very nautical theme to the town - apart from having the North Sea on your doorstep - as the parish church is named after St. Nicholas the patron saint of sailors and children also the site of Lord Horatio Nelson's birth place is only a few miles away in Burnham Thorpe.

To start this trail begin from the Harbour car park, (this car park fills up quickly during the holiday months) go down the narrow street past the Tourist Information Centre to Station road, turn right then immediately left on to High Street. There is a very attractive row of cottages down this road before you reach the junction with Burnt Street/Church Street where you turn right.

Turn left onto Market Lane and follow this track past the cemetery until you reach Cuckoo Lodge.

Cross over the track and continue to the village of Wighton, once over the bridge by the W-W Light Railway Station, follow the road going in the direction of Walsingham.

If you are a little weary after your journey enjoy the return to Wells from Walsingham, on the light railway.

The beautiful village of Little Walsingham has become a place of pilgrimage because in 1061 Lady Richeldis had a vision of the Virgin Mary here and decided to build a replica of the house of Nazareth at the place where a spring was seen in her vision. Many thousands of pilgrims come to the shrine every year and it has become known as 'England's Nazareth'.

Enjoying the Sea breezes at Wells-Next-The-Sea.

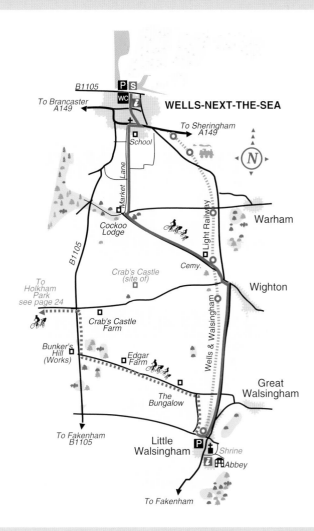

HOLKHAM PARK & MEALS

START & FINISH: Car Park - Lady Ann's Road [S] (opposite the Pottery)

MAP: O.S. Landranger 132 N.W.Norfolk & King's Lynn

LENGTH: (approx)18km (11m) Circular

SURFACE: Stone based grit/metalled

RIDE RATING: Easy adventurous

NOTE: *Inside the grounds of Holkham Park please keep to the estate roadways.*

Holkham Park is situated on the top shoreline of Norfolk, to the east of Burnham Market and west of Wells-Next-The Sea. To the south is Fakenham.

The trail into the Park begins from the car park on Lady Ann's Road. Cross over the A149 and through the gates into Holkham Park. This magnificently parkland with its herd of fallow deer has a wonderfully tranquil atmosphere.

Egyptian and Canadian geese can be seen down on the Lake which is situated beside the majestic 18th century stately mansion of Holkham Hall, once home to the Earls of Leicester.

At the junction of the road beside the Hall take the right hand path, pass the Nursery Gardens to the outer perimeter of the Park. Turn left down the track (Roman Road) to the 'T' junction and turn left and left again back into the park through the South Lodge gates.

Holkham Park.

The South Drive is a very impressive straight road. Go around the Obelisk, and as the drive bends round to the left, stop - take a breather - and feast your eyes on the wonderful panoramic view of the parklands and Holkham Hall.

The sandy track going north from the car park through the Pinewoods on The Meals is a very pleasant ride through the nature reserve that makes up a large part of the coast line of Norfolk. These tall pines along the edge of the sandunes form part of the sea defenses which are very important to the town of Wells.

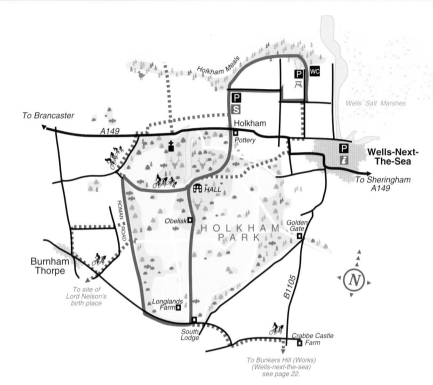

THETFORD FOREST
BRANDON COUNTRY PARK & HIGH LODGE

START & FINISH: Brandon Visitor Centre and High Lodge Car Park

MAP: O.S. Landranger 144 Thetford & Diss

LENGTH: (approx) Brandon trail - 10 ½km (6 ½m) Circular High Lodge trail - 10km (6m) Circular

SURFACE: Forest tracks

RIDE RATING: Easy adventurous

NOTES: *Beware of the flint stones on the forest tracks - they can puncture cycle tyres!*

Thetford Forest is within the Breckland area in the heart of East Anglia, straddling the borders of Norfolk and Suffolk. To the north are the towns of Swaffham and Downham Market and to the south is Thetford and the 'oldest road in Britain' the Ickneild Way. To the west is Ely in the county of Cambridgeshire and to the east is the A1075.

Thetford Forest was planted by the Forestry Commission in 1922 and since that time has become a highly accessible area for leisure activities.

Both the Brandon Park and High Lodge circular cycle routes and are way marked on wide forest tracks. Care must be taken as you cross the busy B1106 between the two cycle routes.

The forest is a haven for many species of wildlife, also from Brandon Country Park Centre there is a 'Tree Trail', where you can be read about different varieties of trees planted within the forest.

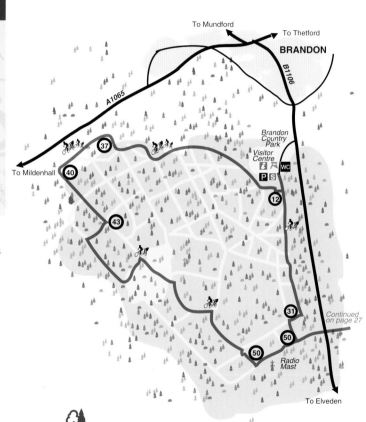

Continued on page 27

Forest Enterprise

Thetford is a working forest - respect warning signs and avoid forest operations and machinery. Always remain alert for forestry vehicles.

To Brandon

Forest Road
(one way)

Lingheath
Farm

B1106

Continued
on page 26

High
Lodge

To Brandon

B1107

To Thetford

Fenced
Experimental
Area

59

62

48

21

28

To Elveden

1 Danger Area

12 Forest Compartments (no's on corner trees)

The cycle trails are waymarked by posts displaying cycle symbols.

ICKNEILD WAY - *KNETTISHALL HEATH*

START: Roundham Heath car park on the A11

FINISH: Euston Hall

MAP: O.S. Landranger 144 Thetford & Diss

LENGTH: (approx) 20km (12 ½m)

SURFACE: Grass/forest tracks/stoney

RIDE RATING: Moderate

NOTE: The Way is well waymarked with a distinctive flint axe emblem and when ever the cyclist's route is separated from the walker's the waymarks and signposts are marked 'Rider's Route' - (Red waymarked arrows for byways, blue for bridleways and white for footpaths).

This section of the Ickneild Way is situated south of the A11 and north of Stanton and the A143. To the west is the A1088 and to the east is the B1111.

The Ickneild Way is a unique long distance path known as 'The Oldest Road in Britain' linking 'The Ridgeway' in Wiltshire, Berkshire and Buckinghamshire and 'Peddar's Way' in Norfolk - total distance 105 miles.

This route begins on the A11 on Roundham Heath going south through Harling Heath towards Knettishall Heath. The Way has been used by travellers and packhorse traffic carrying provisions. The trails history dates back to Neolithic times (2000-4000 BC).

At the A1066 cross over the road and down to Riddlesworth Hall School, follow the road past the church turning right beyond the cottage and after crossing the two fields skirt the woods and ford the Little Ouse River.

Within Knettishall Heath the walker's path begins, it is heralded by a milestone marking the end of Peddar's Way and the beginning of the Ickneild Way.

Cross over the next metalled road and follow the track down to Euston Hall. Before reaching the hall cyclists must take a right hand track to the Knettishall-Euston road. Turn left and follow the road on a wide grass verges to Euston Hall the seat of the Dukes of Grafton.

Within the woodlands there are a wide variety of wild flowers also the greater spotted woodpecker is a frequent visitor.

Village of Euston.

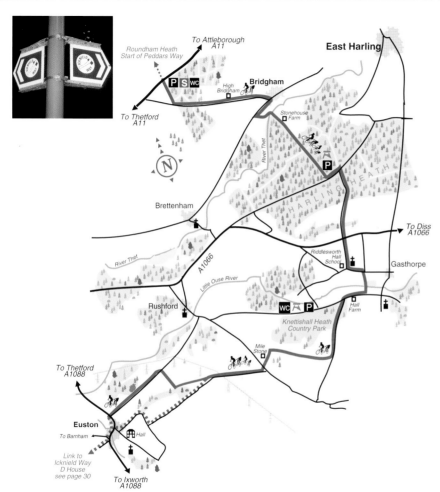

To Attleborough
A11

Roundham Heath
Start of Peddars Way

East Harling

P S WC

High Bridgham
Bridgham

To Thetford
A11

Stonehouse Farm

P

N

H A R L I N G   H E A T H

River Thet

Brettenham

To Diss
A1066

River Thet

A1066

Riddlesworth Hall School

Gasthorpe

Little Ouse River

Rushford

WC P

Hall Farm

Knettishall Heath Country Park

Mile Stone

To Thetford
A1088

Euston

To Barnham

Hall

Link to Icknield Way
D House
see page 30

To Ixworth
A1088

On the Ickneild Way.

ICKNEILD WAY *THE KING'S FOREST*

START & FINISH: Car Park beside the Monument (north of King's Forest) **S**

MAP: O.S. Landranger 144 Thetford & Diss

LENGTH: (approx) Red 15km (9 ¼m) Linear Brown 20km (12 ½m) Circular

SURFACE: Forest tracks/stoney

RIDE RATING: Easy adventurous (both routes)

The Kings Forest is situated south of Thetford Forest and the A11 and north of Bury St Edmunds and the A14. To the west is the A11 and to the east the A134.

Although the Ickneild Way, (the ancient road that boasts 'it is the oldest road in Britain') carries on through the Forest. The red ride is along Seven Tree Road round Berner's Heath through Icklingham and on to Caversham Heath. Iron Age coins have been found around Icklingham and were from the Iceni tribe, Bodicea's countryman and their neighbours the Catuvellauni.

Temple Bridge taking the Way to Caversham Heath was reputed to be the earliest crossing of the River Lark on the old London to Norwich road.

The King's Forest was George V's and planting of this forest by the Forestry Commission began in the year of his 25th Jubilee. The ground is very sandy with pine and broadleaved trees making the forest an excellent habitat for wildlife.

The brown route through the forest along Queen Mary's Avenue is a spectacular ride through ancient Corsican pines and Douglas firs.

At West Stow there is the site of a Saxon Village where sunken-floored huts and a wooden hall have been reconstructed and give a very accurate impression of life in a small Saxon settlement, worth a visit , the site has excellent picnic facilities.

The trail along 'Seven Tree Road' from Icklingham.

To Thetford

To Brandon B1106

Barrow Clump Buildings

Duke's Ride

To Thetford A134

Icknield Way to Euston see page 28

New Zealand Cottages

D House

A11

S P Monument

Berner's Heath

North Stow Hall

P

THE KING'S FOREST

To Newmarket

Seven Tree Road

To Bury St. Edmunds A134

N

Bernersfield Farm

Wordwell

Icklingham

Weatherhill Farm

P

Forest Lodge

P

Culford Park

Culford

Temple Bridge

P Caversham Heath

WC P

West Stow

Icknield Way to Newmarket

Country Park & Visitor Centre

Lackford

To Bury St. Edmunds A1101

Route through King's Forest.

ALTON WATER

START & FINISH: Visitors Centre **S**

MAP: O.S. Landranger 169 Ipswich & The Naze

LENGTH: (approx) 13km (8m) Circular

SURFACE: Stone base/metalled/grass

RIDE RATING: Visitor Centre to the Bridge - Easy From the Bridge via Birchwood car park. Moderate From the Bridge across Alton Water via Tattingstone back to the centre.

Alton Water is situated in the country of Suffolk, east of the A137, and west of the town on Holbrook and the B1080 on the Shotley Peninsular. To the north is Ipswich and to the south is the estuary of the River Stour.

The tranquillity of Suffolk stretches to the shores of Alton Water which is set in over 400 acres of wonderful countryside. This reservoir was built in 1978 to provide water for Ipswich.

The track around the perimeter of the reservoir is reasonably flat on the south side - but the track along the north shore of the water is definitely more energetic!

There is plenty of fishing (by permit) along the water's edge and in the autumn and winter huge pike can be caught - twenty pounders (not just a fisherman's tale!).

![View across the River Stour to Harwich.]

View across the River Stour to Harwich.

START & FINISH: Lower Holbrook Village car park(or Alton Water Visitor Centre car park for an alternative start point) **S**

MAP: O.S. Landranger 169 Ipswich & The Naze

LENGTH: (approx) 13km (8m) Circular

SURFACE: Metalled

RIDE RATING: Moderate

The Stour Estuary has been designated an area of Outstanding Natural Beauty where many species of waders and wildfowl can be spotted.

The Shotley Peninsular is situated east of the A137 Manningtree to Ipswich road. This finger of land is bordered to the north by the River Orwell and to the south by the River Stour converging at Shotley Gate before flowing into the North Sea.

Should you start from Alton Water you will cycle past the Royal Hospital School with its imposing tower, which was built in 1712 for the orphans of sailors and the children of wounded sailors. - The Indian princeling figurehead of HMS Ganges stands on this site whilst the mast off the Ganges is now in use by the Suffolk Constabulary in Shotley.

The start of this trail is from the car park at Lower Holbrook and follows the country lanes and bridleways around the peninsular. Beside the 'Baker's Arms' at Harkstead there are outstanding views over the River Stour to Harwich and to The North sea beyond Felixstowe.

Once past Erwarton Church - where it is said within the walls there is a casket containing the heart of Anne Boleyn, one of Henry VIII's wives - and Erwarton Hall with its splendid gatehouse, take the bridleway on your left as the road turns the corner to the right. At Crouch House follow the lane to a 'T' junction and turn right to Holbrook. At Holbrook Gardens turn left and left again back to Lower Holbrook.

STANTON

START & FINISH: Red Stanton Brown Hopton [S]

MAP: O.S. Landranger 144 Thetford & Diss

LENGTH: (approx) Red 18km (11m) Circular
Brown 11km (6 ¾m) Circular

SURFACE: Metalled/stoney/grass

RIDE RATING: Both routes Easy Adventurous

NOTE: Both these routes are way marked with green signs and arrows with a windmill logo.

These routes are situated south of Garholdisham and the A1066 and north of Ixworth. To the west is the A1088 and the village of Coney Weston and to the east lies the villages of Wattisfield, Hinderclay and Thelnetham.

Both these trails use old trackways and green lanes which connected the hamlets and villages, also the ancient drove roads which are now only used by the farmers for access and leisure walkers and riders

The Red route begins at Stanton car park and and goes north west out of the town on the A143 for half a mile before turning left onto a track (George Lane). Turning right on the Barningham Road. Once under the pylons turn right onto the bridleway to Home farm. Turn left in Barningham to Hepworth passing Reeves Hall. On your return to Stanton you will pass the Windmill which is the logo for the waymark arrows.

The Brown route begins in Hopton car park. Turn right and immediately past the church (on your left) turn right onto a track before picking up the by-way to Weather Cock Farm. Turn right onto the road after Ward's Farm turn right onto a bridleway. Follow the waymarket arrows down to Hepworth before returning via Reeves Hall and Market Weston.

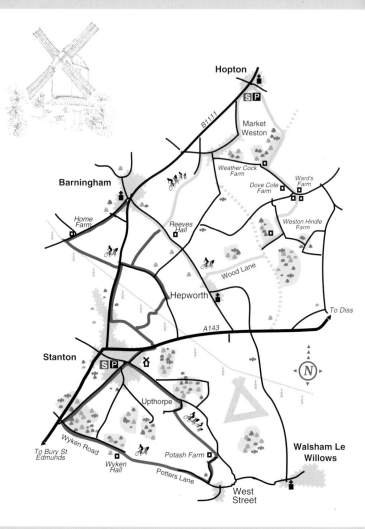

THE THREE FOREST TRAIL
RENDLESHAM & TUNSTALL FORESTS

START & FINISH: Rendlesham Forest cycle hire car park **S**

MAP: O.S. Landranger 169 Ipswich & 156 Saxmundum

LENGTH: (approx) Rendlesham Trail 12km (7 ¹/₂m) Circular Tunstall Trail 14 ¹/₂km (9m) Circular Connecting road 3km (2m)

SURFACE: Forest track/metalled/sandy

RIDE RATING: Easy adventurous

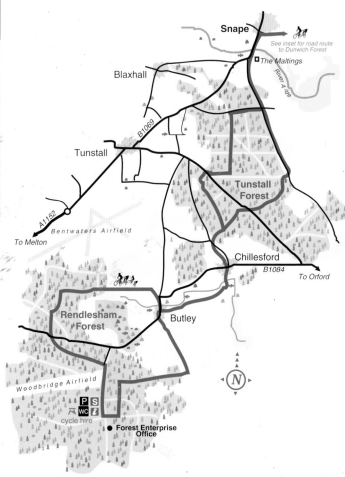

These two forests are situated south of the A1094 and north of Felixstowe and the River Deben. To the west is Woodbridge and the A1152 to the east is the River Alde and the north sea coast.

The forest tracks are wide and in some cases metalled, due to the sandy ground any rain tends to drain leaving the forest trail quite dry.

During the 'Great Storm' of October 1987 the winds blew down half the trees within the forests which gave an ideal opportunity to use the wide tracks as open rides and replant some of the areas with broad leaf trees rather than all Suffolk corsican pines.

The regeneration of the heathland has benefited the wildlife, and where ponds have been created the wetter areas have assisted the forest animals.

The route through the forest tracks, over the heathlands and through the purple heather between the two forest areas make this trail a very enjoyable ride.

It is worth diverting to the village of Orford on the River Alde with its majestic Norman Keep as the panoramic view from top of the Castle looking over the coast is breathtaking.

The connecting road between these two forests and Dunwich Forest go through the villages of Snape and Thorpeness. Snape stands on the bank of the River Alde with its famous Maltings concert hall. and Thorpeness with its mock Tudor water tower on stilts 'The House in the Clouds'.

Close by is the nature reserve of North Warren together with The Meare a large recreational boating lake.

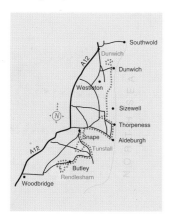

This map shows the connecting route for cyclist who wish to ride the THREE FOREST TRAIL.

See page 38/39 for Dunwich forest trail.

One of the sandy tracks through the forest.

THE THREE FOREST TRAIL
DUNWICH FOREST

START & FINISH: Dunwich Forest car park [S]

MAP: O.S. Landranger 156 Saxmundham

LENGTH: (approx) 7km (4 ½m) Circular
Connecting road from Tunstall 20km (12 ½m)

SURFACE: Forest track/metalled/grass

RIDE RATING: Forest - Easy. Connecting route -
Easy Adventurous

Dunwich Forest is to the east of the B1125 and west of the North Sea coast. To the north is Southwold and the A1095 with Dunwich Heath to the south.

In the 12th century Dunwich was a large city but over the next 400 years nearly all was lost to the sea, as the cliffs fell due to erosion of the coastline.

The trail from Eastbridge over the heather covered heathland to Dunwich is very enjoyable on wide sandy paths and wooded tracks. At the junction with the road before turning into Dunwich it is worth visiting Dunwich Heath, now owned by the National Trust, it is a lovely spot for a picnic before tackling the forest trail north of Dunwich village.

The route through Dunwich Forest amongst the tall pines is a very pleasant one, a good circular trail round lots of bends, but no hills!

The North Sea coast at Dunwich Heath.

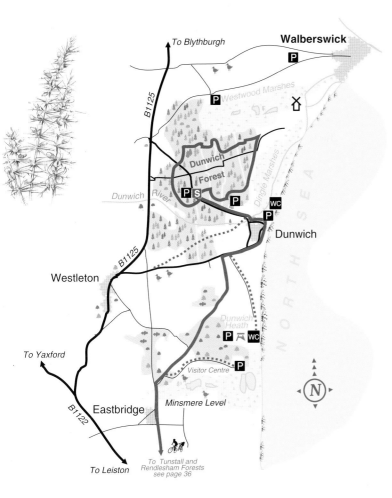

To Blythburgh

Walberswick

B1125

Westwood Marshes

Dunwich Forest

Dunwich River

B1125

Westleton

To Yaxford

B1122

Eastbridge

Dingle Marshes

WC

Dunwich

NORTH SEA

Dunwich Heath

WC

Visitor Centre

Minsmere Level

To Tunstall and
Rendlesham Forests
see page 36

To Leiston

N

The forest is home to a variety of wildlife, the Red, fallow and muntjac deer can often be sighted but although there are many foxes, rabbits and hares, unless you are up early in the day, they would escape being seen.

The water courses attract many species of dragonfly and where you see the wild honeysuckle growing the white admiral butterfly can be found in abundance.

Dunwich Forest.

DEBENHAM

START & FINISH: Red Debenham
Brown Clowes's Corner

MAP: O.S. Landranger 156 Saxmundum

LENGTH: (approx) Red 7km (4 ½m) Circular
Brown 6km (3 ¾m) Circular

SURFACE: Metalled/stoney/grass

RIDE RATING: Easy (both routes)

These two routes are situated east of Debenham and the B1071
and west of Earl Soham and the A1120. The A1120 also runs
south of the trails with the villages of Kenton and
Monk Soham to the north.

Debenham was a thriving wool centre, as depicted on its village sign, and used to be on the old direct route between Norwich and Ipswich. The inhabitants complained even then (beginning of the last century!) of the heavy traffic.

The Red trail begins from the car park in Debenham and is waymarked with green signs and arrows. At Priory Lane turn right and right again onto a bridleway to Mill Farm and the junction with Kenton Road. The route is along both delightful green lanes and wide bridleway tracks this has been marked for both walkers and cyclists. Crows Hall is an imposing moated 16th century brick-built manor house with a range of outbuildings onced used by the Royalist cavalry in the Civil War.

The Brown trail starts at Clowes's Corner and is an extension of route one from Waddlegoose Lane (also known as Waddledickie - Suffolk dialect for 'donkey'). This trail is on a 'B' road between the start and Ashfield Cum Thorpe and country lanes thereafter

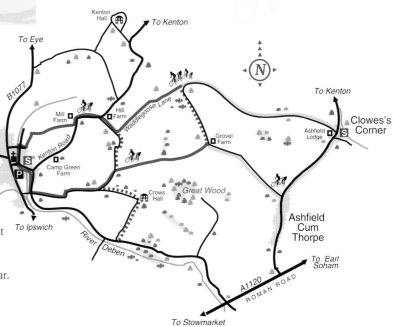

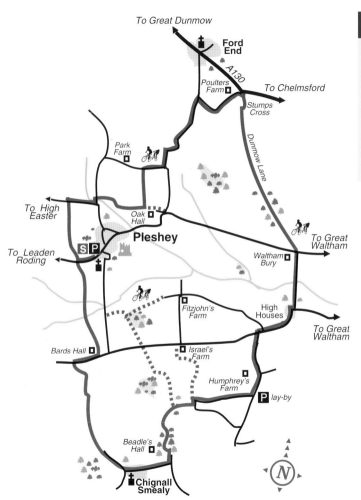

PLESHEY

START & FINISH: Car park, Pleshey **S**

MAP: O.S. Landranger 167 Chelmsford & Harow

LENGTH: (approx) 14km (8 ³/₄m) Circular

SURFACE: Metalled/stoney/grass

RIDE RATING: Easy adventurous

Pleshey is situated west of the B186 / A1060 and to the east by the A130. North of Pleshey is Great Dunmow and to the south is Chelmsford.

The route is mainly on wide bridleway tracks and very pleasant country lanes.

The remains of the Norman castle on Pleshey is one of the best surviving earthworks in England. The village is surrounded by a ditch and bank and inside this a 50ft high castle mound and its moat, unfortunately there is no longer a castle but only a 15th century red-brick bridge spanning the moat.

In 1397 the Duke of Gloucester was heard trying to overthrow King Richard 11, where upon the Duke was lured from Pleshey and taken to Calais where he was murdered by assassins.

The start of this circular route is from the village of Pleshey and takes you clockwise round some of Essex's exellent bridleways. On leaving the car park in Pleshey turn right onto the bridleway going north of the village.

The wide bridleway with its tall hedges Dunmow Lane between Stumps Cross and Waltham Bury was once the main road between Chelmsford and Great Dunmow.

BASILDON *LANGDON HILLS COUNTRY PARK*

START & FINISH: Red Visitor Centre, Dunton
Brown One Tree Hill Country Park

MAP: O.S. Landranger 178 Thames Estuary

LENGTH: (approx) Red 9km (5 ¾m) Circular
Brown 7km (4 ½m) Circular

SURFACE: Metalled/stoney/forest tracks

RIDE RATING: Moderate

These two rides are situated south of the A127 and the town of Basildon in Essex, and north of the A13. To the west lies the M25 and the village of Bulphan, whilst to the east is Vange.

Basildon became of the eight new towns build near London after World War 2 to provide homes for the City's growing population. In Dunton Hills a bungalow has been restored to its original condition, very interesting and worth a visit. This Estate was saved as a nature reserve when most of the other old Plotlands were redeveloped.

Enjoy the wide plotland roads through to Lincewood where close-by on the recreational ground there are thousands of Green-tipped orchids during the months of May and June. There are superb views looking towards London over the River Thames estuary.

In the woods on Marks Hill, if you stop and listen carefully you can hear the tapping sound of the Green, Great Spotted and Lesser Spotted woodpeckers.

The trail circumnavigates One Tree Hill in the Country Park before going around Willow Park which is a haven for dragonflies and butterflies hovering over the ponds in the rough grassland.

The Essex Wildlife Trust owns more than 80 nature reserves of which this is one.

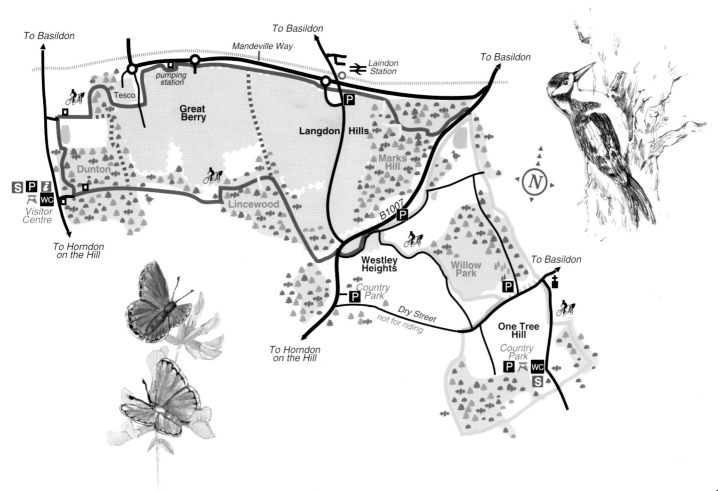

To Basildon

Mandeville Way

To Basildon

To Basildon

pumping
station

Tesco

Laindon
Station

P

Great
Berry

Langdon Hills

Dunton

Marks
Hill

S P i

WC

Visitor
Centre

Lincewood

B1007

P

N

To Horndon
on the Hill

To Basildon

Westley
Heights

Willow
Park

Country
Park

P

P

Dry Street
not for riding

To Horndon
on the Hill

One Tree
Hill

Country
Park

P

WC

S

BARDFIELD SALING

START & FINISH: Red Car park beside Andrewsfield Airfield Brown Shalford Green   S

MAP: O.S. Landranger 167 Chelmsford & Harlow

LENGTH: (approx) Red 9km (5 ½m) Circular Brown 8km (5m) Circular

SURFACE: Metalled/stoney tracks

RIDE RATING: Red Easy adventurous Brown Easy adventurous/Moderate

NOTES: On the Brown route between Park Hall and Hunt's Farm look carefully for bridleway signs to get across the field.

These two routes are north of the A120 and south of Great Bardfield. To the west is Stebbing and Great Dunmow and to the east is Braintree.

The Red route begins beside the Airfield of Andrewsfield, which during World War 2 was an American base with B-26 Marauders. At the end of 1945 the airfield was virtualy deserted, the concrete runways disappeared and a grass landing strop was laid. In 1976 the airfield was officially licensed and it is now used for small civil and private aircraft.

Turning right from the car park the route takes you over country lanes and bridleways and is one of the nicest routes with a variety of woodland and open countryside to ride through.

The Brown route, a circular route from Shalford Green does also begin and end on country lanes, with the middle part being on bridleways/byways alongside fields, which can tend to be muddy and in some cases (especially if you take the bridleway from Park Hall to Great Bardfield) quite difficult depending what the farmer has sown that season.

Windmill at Gt. Bardfield.

B-26 Marauder of
the US Airforce.

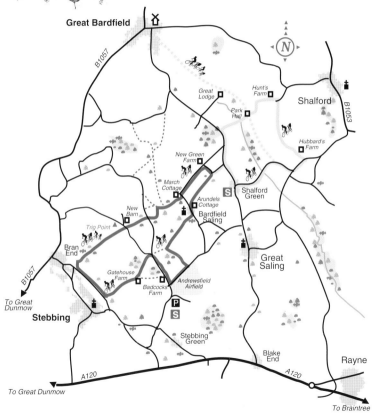

Great Bardfield

B1057

Great
Lodge

Hunt's
Farm

Shalford

B1053

Park
Hall

Hubbard's
Farm

New Green
Farm

March
Cottage

Arundels
Cottage

S

Shalford
Green

New
Barn

Bardfield
Saling

Trig Point

Bran
End

B1057

Great
Saling

Gatehouse
Farm

Andrewsfield
Airfield

Badcocks
Farm

P
S

To Great
Dunmow

Stebbing

Stebbing
Green

Blake
End

Rayne

A120

A120

To Great Dunmow

To Braintree

N

Andrewsfield Airfield.

FLITCH WAY *GREAT DUNMOW - TILEKILN GREEN*

START: Start at Greencroft [S]

FINISH: Tilekiln Green

MAP: O.S. Landranger 167 Chelmsford & Harlow

LENGTH: (approx) 8km (5m) Linear

SURFACE: Stone base grit/grass

RIDE RATING: Easy

NOTE: Flitch Way can be ridden from Braintree through to Tilekiln Green but due to the length of the route we have made two trails with a connecting route to save going on the A120 and through Great Dunmow (as the path out of Gt. Dunmow is a footpath only).

Flitch Way is situated in Essex to the east of Bishop's Stortford and the M11 and west of Braintree. Great Dunmow is the mid-way town on the route. Along the northside of the Way lies the A120. South and near the western end of the trail is Hatfield Forest

The name of the Way comes from a medieval Flitch Ceremony held in the village of Little Dunmow. this ceremony was originally set up by Augustinian monks - and involved giving a 'flitch' (a large piece of bacon) to couples who had not argued in marriage for a year and a day!

Flitch Way follows the old track bed of the former Bishop's Stortford to Braintree railway. The single track opened in the 1800's and was used mainly by local people going to market.

Small tank engines worked the line which was closed for passengers in 1852 but carried on being used for goods traffic until 1969.

Begin this section of Flitch Way from Greencroft off the A120, tt is a superb ride. Once you have passed the village of Takeley, on your left running alongside the trail, is the Royal Forest of Hatfield. Originally owned by the Crown and now by the

National Trust the history of the forest, like many of the ancient trees growing here, go back many hundreds of years.

The different varieties of wild plants and in season, the butterflies you will encounter along this track are in abundance.

The trail ends at an old railway bridge in the village of Tilekiln Green two miles from the centre of Bishop's Stortford.

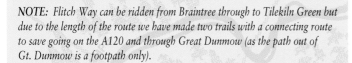

LInk to Braintree/Gt.Dunmo section page 47

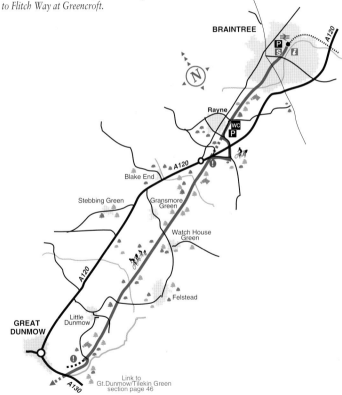

...onnecting route (red dotted) for those who have cycled through from ...aintree (Connecting mileage 9km (5 ¹/₂m) ❶ Cross over the A130 turn ...ht onto the smaller road on the left called the Chelmsford Road, carry ... up this road turning on to the first road on your left, at the ...ndabout take your first left and cycle past Clapton Hall. When you ...ch the B184 turn left and almost immediately turn right to Bacon ...d. Follow this meandering lane into Highcross Lane East and back ... to Flitch Way at Greencroft.

BRAINTREE

Rayne

Blake End

Stebbing Green

Gransmore Green

Watch House Green

Felstead

Little Dunmow

GREAT DUNMOW

Link to Gt.Dunmow/Tilekin Green section page 46

START: Braintree Station car park **S**

FINISH: Great Dunmow on the A130

MAP: O.S. Landranger 167 Chelmsford & Harlow

LENGTH: (approx) 13km (8m) Linear

SURFACE: Stoney/grass

RIDE RATING: Easy

NOTES: At Rayne look for signs for optional route rather than crossing the A120

The first stage of this route from Braintree to Rayne Station is very well surfaced and therefore instead of concentrating on where you are cycling, you can enjoy the surrounding countryside.

Rayne Station has been renovated and is now a visitor centre. On leaving the Station (*it is advisable to take the alternative route to avoid crossing the very busy A120*) turn left and cross over Flitch Way cycle straight down the lane turning right onto Mill Lane, the lane takes you back on to Flien Way where you turn left and carry on cycling to Little Dunmow. Half a mile after Little Dunmow there

is a bridge with a Byway crossing your trail ❶ turn left onto this track and follow it until you meet the A130 Great Dunmow to Chelmsford road, turning right for the town of Great Dunmow.

If you are cycling to the end of Flitch Way at Tilekiln Green Turn left off the A130 onto a lane called The Chelmsford Road (*connecting route red dotted described on page 46*)

HATFIELD FOREST

START & FINISH: Country Park car park **S**
(N.T. car park charge)

MAP: O.S. Landranger 167 Chelmsford & Harlow

LENGTH: (approx) 6km (3 ¾m) Circular

SURFACE: Grass/forest track

RIDE RATING: Easy

NOTES: Cyclists are welcome in the forest and are reminded that it is an area of great importance for wildlife - bicycles are not permitted in the Gravel Pit or in the Lake Area.

Hatfield Forest is situation in Essex, south of the A120 and Stanstead Airport and north of Hatfield Heath and the A1060. To the west is the Bishop's Stortford and the M11 and to the east is the B183 Takeley to Hatfield Heath road.

Earl Harold once owned the great Forest of Essex, but it was Henry 1 who introduced fallow deer to this country. Hatfield was one of those chosen places, and given the name 'forest' as at the time the word meant 'a place for deer'. In 1238 the Forest passed into private hands, and in 1446 the monarchy relinquished its right to the deer. In 1924 the land was handed over to the National Trust by the Buxton family.

THE NATIONAL TRUST

Hatfield Forest.

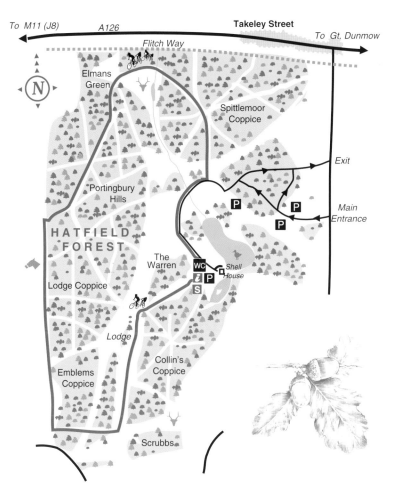

To M11 (J8) A126 **Takeley Street** To Gt. Dunmow

Flitch Way

N

Elmans Green

Spittlemoor Coppice

Exit

Portingbury Hills

Main Entrance

H A T F I E L D F O R E S T

The Warren

WC

Shell House

Lodge Coppice

Lodge

Collin's Coppice

Emblems Coppice

Scrubbs

Within the 1,049 acres that comprise of grassland a lake and forest, there are today approx. 250 in the fallow deer herd, and about 60 of the more recent inhabitant the muntjac deer which can often be seen grazing in the woodland. There are a wide variety of plants such as violets, ground ivy and wood sorrel that inhabit the woodland floor which flower early in the season before the trees' leaves cut out the light.

Many of the pollarded trees (oak, ash, hornbeam and hawthorn trees that have been cut high up out of reach of the deer and allowed to regrow, giving them a squat knobbly shape) often grow to the age of 400 years old - they could tell a few stories!

At Portingbury Hills there are ditches and banks which are the remains of an Iron Age settlement.

LITTLE EASTON *THAXTED - BAMBER GREEN*

START & FINISH: Red Little Easton Car Park **S** beside the Church Brown Thaxted car park

MAP: O.S. Landranger 167 Chelmsford & Harlow

LENGTH: (approx) Red 7km (4 ½m) Circular
Brown 14km (8 ¾m) Circular

SURFACE: Red Metalled/concrete/stoney
Brown Metalled

RIDE RATING: Easy Adventurous

The routes in the area from Thaxted to Little Easton are situated north of the A120 and Great Dunmow. West of the B184 and east of Stanstead Airport and the M11.

This peaceful countryside aroundLittle Easton and the great estate of the Maynard family of Easton Lodge must have been shattered during World War II as this land north west of Gt. Dunmow was deemed suitable by the Secretary of State for War as a US airfield. A beautiful stained glass window commemorating the US airman was commisioned in the Little Easton church at the end of the war.

The Red route - a circular trail from Little Easton via Bamber's Green. With your back to the church in Little Easton cycle down the road over a bridge, beside a thatched cotttage on your right, to a signpost at the end of a copse of trees *(be careful - there is a bridleway signpost before this going into the woods - it is misleading).* The path goes close to the fence around the edge of the trees and across the field. In the field (depending on the season) of waving goldern ears of grain you will find a concrete track ahead of you which is the remains of Great Dunmow airfield.

Windmill at Thaxted.

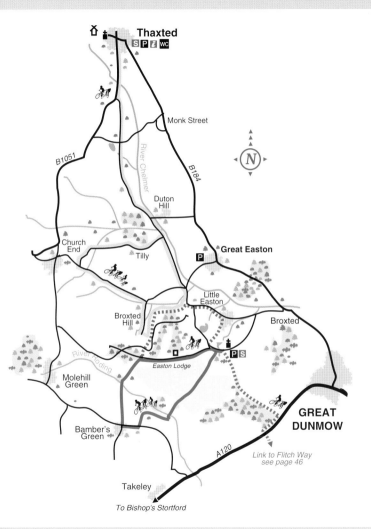

Thaxted
S P i wc

Monk Street

B1051

River Chelmer

B184

Duton Hill

N

Church End

Tilly

Great Easton
P

Little Easton

Broxted Hill

Broxted

Easton Lodge
P S

Molehill Green

River Roding

Bamber's Green

GREAT DUNMOW

A120

Link to Flitch Way
see page 46

Takeley

To Bishop's Stortford

Thaxted village centre.

Follow the bridleway over the old airstrips down to a bridge over a stream to the little village of Bamber's Green. Turn right at the road, and right again at the bridleway signpost just after the telephone box.

As a track crosses your bridleway coming out the woods on your left, turn right and continue past Easton Lodge back to Little Easton.

The Brown route begins in the ancient town of Thaxted with its recorded history dating back to before the Domesday Book. Approach the town from any point and you are overshadowed by the 181ft high spire of the beautiful parish church. The composer Gustav Holst lived in the centre of the town where you can also see the old timber framed building of the Guildhall built by the Cutler's guild in 1390. John Webbs, wonderful Windmill can be seen on the outskirts of the town past a row of restored almshouses and a very well kept cemetery.

Once through the town take the B1051 Broxted road for 1/2 mile until you turn off to the left onto a country lane down to Duton Hill and Little Easton. This very pleasant and attractive lane follows the River Chelmer as it flows through Little Easton and eventually into the North Sea via Chelmsford.

THE BELCHAMPS

START & FINISH: Lay-Bye on the B1064 **S** near Pentlow parish church

MAP: O.S. Landranger 155 Bury St Edmunds

LENGTH: (approx) 20km (12 ½m) Circular

SURFACE: Metalled/grass/stoney

RIDE RATING: Moderate adventurous

This route is situated south of the A1092 and the River Stour in the north eastern limit of the county of Essex. To the east is Sudbury and Long Melford and to the west is Stoke by Clare and Great Yeldham.

This country ride is on a mixture of quite lanes and very pleasant bridleways, also a ride through the middle of a field - luckily the crop had been harvested when we cycled it!

To start the trail keep the round towered parish church of Pentlow on your right (there are only six churches in Essex with a circular tower), cross over the road onto a bridleway beside a stable, follow the path through the woods to the road where you turn left then right beside a pumping station (small brick building). Continue along the track, under the power lines,

turning to go down hill in the middle of the field to the bank of the River Stour.

Once past Claredown Farm turn left on to the by-way, a gradual climb to the 'T' junction - there are a wonderful variety of wild flowers along this tree lined track - turn left for Belchamp St Paul.

After a well earned rest with a picnic on the village green, and you feel like saving your strength for another days ride - take a short cut (red dotted line) back through Pentlow. Otherwise turn right at the signpost onto the

Trail beside the River Stour.

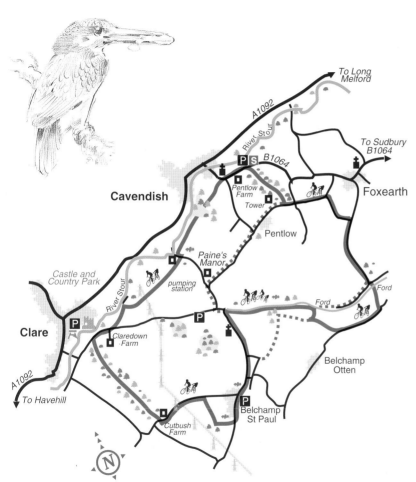

bridleway across a field, beware if it has rained this route can be boggy. At the road junction turn left and follow the lane to Pentlow.

Before reaching the village of Pentlow turn right onto a by-way beside Pentlow Tower which stands 90ft high and was built in 1859 by Edward Bull in memorial to his parents.

Pentlow Church.

CLAVERING

START & FINISH: Clavering Town **S**

MAP: O.S. Landranger 167 Chelmsford & Harlow

LENGTH: (approx) 21km (13m) Circular

SURFACE: Metalled/Stone base tracks/grass

RIDE RATING: Moderate

This trail east of Clavering is situated east of the M11. The B1038 is to the north and Bishop's Stortford to the south.

The route is down country lanes, on by-ways and bridleways over the undulating hills of west Essex.

In the middle of the town of Clavering, overlooking the ford, is Chestnut cottage which is the smallest house in Essex, only 8ft wide and 10ft from front to back, a ladder is used to go upstairs.

The ground in this area of Essex is very different from the rest of the county, deep under the soil there is a chalk layer that isn't visible, but due to the rivers Stort and Cam having cut through the hills they have uncovered the chalk on the sides of the valley.

Due to this phenomena there are many wild flowers that love this chalky soil such as Marjoram and Traveller's Joy which grow in abundance in this part of Essex. The beautiful purplish flowers of wild Marjoram can be seen down the lanes and in the hedgebanks north of Berden in Parsonage Lane, this flower was a symbol of happiness used in years gone by for crowning wedding couples.

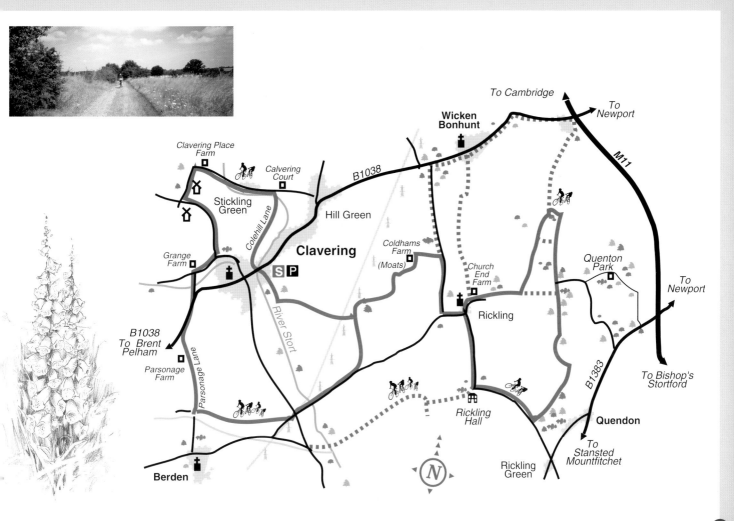

To Cambridge

To Newport

Wicken
Bonhunt

M11

Clavering Place
Farm

Calvering
Court

B1038

Stickling
Green

Colehill Lane

Hill Green

Clavering

Coldhams
Farm
(Moats)

Church
End
Farm

Quenton
Park

Grange
Farm

S P

River Stort

Rickling

To
Newport

B1038
To Brent
Pelham

Parsonage Lane

Parsonage
Farm

B1383

To Bishop's
Stortford

Rickling
Hall

Quendon

To
Stansted
Mountfitchet

Berden

N

Rickling
Green

COLCHESTER

START & FINISH: Beacon End (Grime's Dyke) **S**

MAP: O.S. Landranger 168 Colchester

LENGTH: (approx) 14km (8 ¾m) Circular

SURFACE: Metalled/stoney

RIDE RATING: Easy adventurous

The route is situated in Essex between Stanway and the A12 to the north and Layer de la Haye and Abberton Reservoir to the south. To the west is the town of Marks Tey and to the east is Colchester.

This trail is along the ancient Grime's Dyke and the quiet lanes and bridleways of this picturesque district of Colchester. It begins at Beacon End on the bridleway along Gryme's Dyke. This Dyke runs to the west of Camulodunum (Roman name for Colchester) thought to have formed a defence system between the River Colne and the Roman River in a large 12 mile rectangle. They were built by the British well before the Romans came to these shores. The dyke is in places 50ft deep. 'Gryme' is the old name for the Devil and as this dyke was so large it was thought to have been worked by him.

The route continues along bridleways and quiet lanes. Having passed Birch Hall on the return route and continued on the tracks through the woods and open countryside the bridleway crosses the B1022, if you turn left at this road junction (about a quarter of a mile) you will come to the entrance of Cochester Zoo, well worth a visit. Otherwise cross the road and continue along the bridleway to Grime's Dyke.

Map labels (left)

To Colchester

WITHAM

S
P

A12

To Chalmsford

A12

B1018

Blue Mills

Wickam Bishops

Wickam Hall

River Blackwater

B1019

Langford

River Chelmer

A414

To Chelmsford

MALDON

WC
P

Heybridge Basin

P WC

(N)

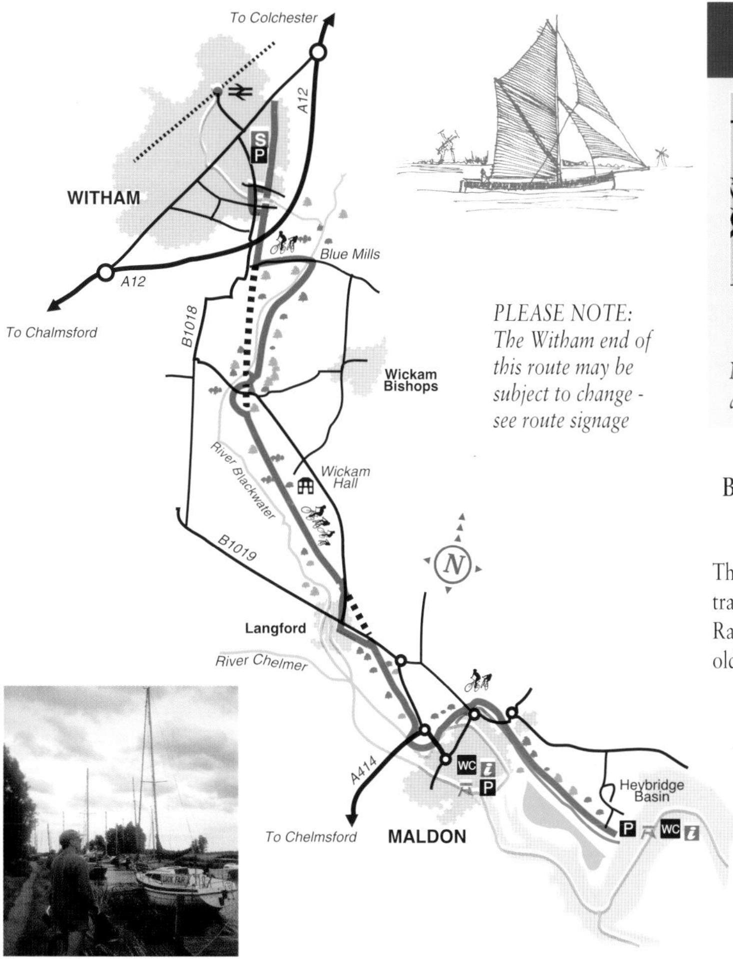

PLEASE NOTE:
The Witham end of
this route may be
subject to change -
see route signage

Moorings on the River Blackwater.

BLACKWATER TRAIL
WITHAM - MALDON - HEYBRIDGE BASIN

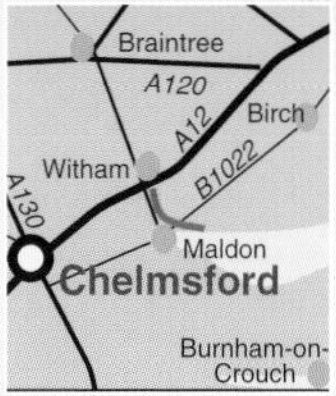

Braintree
A120
Birch
A120
Witham
B1022
A130
Maldon
Chelmsford
Burnham-on-Crouch

START: Witham on the B1018 **S**

FINISH: Heybridge Basin, Maldon

MAP: O.S. Landranger 168 Colchester

LENGTH: (approx) 15km (9 ¼m) Linear

SURFACE: Metalled/stoney/grass

RIDE RATING: Easy adventurous

NOTES: *The section from Malson to the Estuary along the canal towpath is approximately 6km (3 ¾m) in length*

This trail is situated in Essex south of Witham following the River Blackwater to the estuary at Maldon. To the west is the B1019 and to the east is the village of Wickham Biships.

The trail out of Witham follows the old trackbed of the former Witham-Maldon Railway. Where parts of the old railway track are still in private ownership the trail follows the country lanes, and all access points are marked clearly along the route.

From the track alongside the by-pass follow the path down to the canal towpath and turning left you will reach the outskirts of Malden, continue along the canal bank on a long straight stretch to Heybridge Basin where there are plenty of opportunities for refreshments in the cafes along the estuary wall - watching the river as it flows out into the North Sea.

Maldon on the river Blackwater is a historic market town and has been a port for a 1,000 years. Traditional Thames Barges moor in the picturesque Hythe Quay.

RIVER LEE COUNTRY PARK

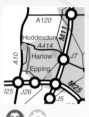

START & FINISH: Broxbourne - Country
Park car park [S]

MAP: O.S. Landranger 166 Luton & Hereford

LENGTH: (approx)14km (8 ¾m) Circular

SURFACE: Stone base grit/grass

RIDE RATING: Easy

NOTE: The route shown on this map may be subject to change as further tracks are made available for cyclists.

River Lee Navigation.

The River Lee Country Park is situated between the towns of Broxbourne in Hertfordshire and Waltham Abbey in Essex. to the west is the A10 and to the east is the B194 to Lower Nazeing.

Lee Valley Park was established in 1967 to help the people of London enjoy a 23 mile leisure route through the green corridor of the Lee and Stort Navigation system from the City of London to Essex and Hertfordshire. It was created to regenerate 10,000 acres of land and water for a wide range of leisure activities and for nature conservation.

This trail is totally off-road on flat tracks skirting the lakes and rivers and through parkland, a wonderfully scenic area with an amazing amount of water fowl and wildlife both on and off the rivers and lakes. The area is renowned for the varieties of orchids that can be seen in spring and dragonflies and damselflies in summer.

From the car park at the start of the trail follow the well signposted cycling route, along the way there are ample picnic areas and seats along the river to sit back and enjoy the swans and other water birds paddling quietly up and down the river.

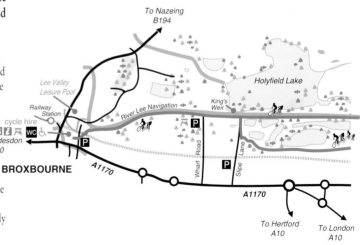

If you want to extend your ride along the towpath of the River Lee Navigation down to the City of London it is advisable to buy the Lee Valley Map and to contact the Countryside Centre on 01992 713838 for access availability.

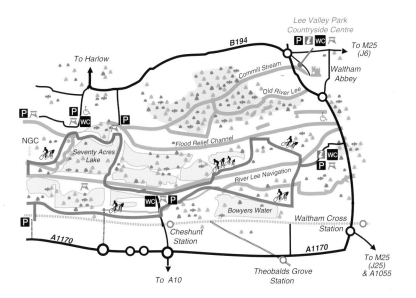

EPPING FOREST

START & FINISH: Information Centre Epping Forest [S]

MAP: O.S. Landranger 177 East London

LENGTH: (approx) 15km (9 ¼m) Circular

SURFACE: Forest tracks/metalled

RIDE RATING: Moderate

NOTES: *Care must be taken whilst cycling on the bridleways as there are serveral major roads running through the forest.*

Epping Forest in Essex is situated west of the River Lee Navigation and the A112 and east of Loughton and M11. South of the town of Epping and the M25 and north of Chingford.

This ancient forest south of Epping covers an area of 6000 acres and since 1878, when the Epping Forest Act was passed, control of the Forest was placed in the hands of the City of London where one third is now grazing land.

The first Royal forests in England were set up by William the Conqueror where he declared that all wildlife and the inhabitands of the forest would be protected by law.

Within the Forest there is a vast timber framed hunting Lodge which can still be seen today, was originally commissioned by Henry VIII and known as the Great Standing. In 1602

Queen Elizabeth I regularly hunted on horseback within the forest and used the Great Standing which was then known as the Queen Elizabeth's Hunting Lodge.

A trail through this beautiful forest of old oak and beech trees is an exhilarating experience, and although we have indicated a circular route using bridleways and roads within the forest, there are so many tracks through the woodland glades you will have no difficulty enjoying any distance you feel like undertaking.

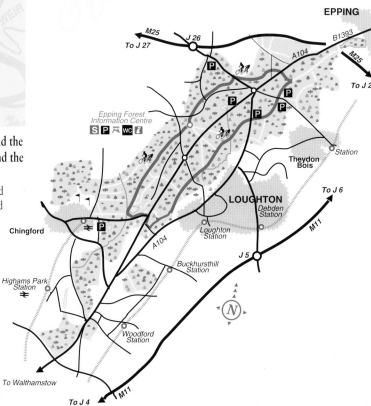

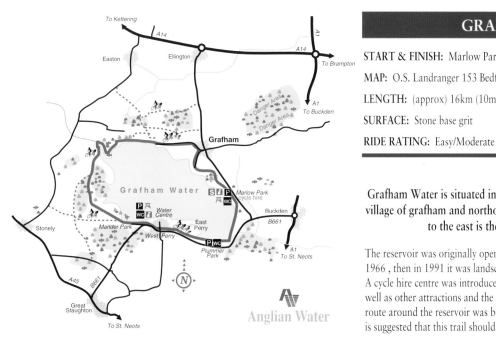

GRAFHAM WATER

START & FINISH: Marlow Park car park

MAP: O.S. Landranger 153 Bedford & Huntingdon

LENGTH: (approx) 16km (10m) Circular

SURFACE: Stone base grit

RIDE RATING: Easy/Moderate

Grafham Water is situated in the Cambridgeshire south of the A14 and the village of grafham and northof the A45. To the west is Kimbolton Park and to the east is the A1 and the town of Brampton.

The reservoir was originally opened in 1966 , then in 1991 it was landscaped - A cycle hire centre was introduced as well as other attractions and the cycle route around the reservoir was born. It is suggested that this trail should be ridden anti-clockwise to avoid crossing the road section at Perry.

All the way around the route stays reasonabley close to the waters edge offering spectacular views of the water and the wildlife that uses it.

RUTLAND WATER

START & FINISH: Whitwell Park car park **S**

MAP: O.S. Explorer 15 Rutland Water

LENGTH: (approx) 26 ¼km (17m) Circular
Including the Peninsular 40km (25m)

SURFACE: Stone base grit/grass/metalled

RIDE RATING: Easy /Moderate

NOTE: It is suggested that the route is cycled anti-clockwise to avoid crossing the road between Manton and Lyndon.

Rutland Water is situated in the County of Leicestershire. The town of Oakham and the A6003 are to the west, with Stamford and the A1 to the east. To the north is the A606, with the A47 to the south.

Rutland Water was originally in the historic county of Rutland and is one of western Europe's largest man-made lakes covering 3100 acres. It was completed in 1977 to supply water to the towns and cities in the West Midlands.

Exploring the route beside Rutland Water, whether you take in the peninsular section or not, is a very pleasurable experience, especially with the wonderful view of the lake as you cycle round. The route is mainly off-road and although the majority of this trail is reasonably flat there are a couple of hills to negotiate - you may need to find a refreshment stop after your climb! and enjoy a rest at one of the picnic areas.

There are nature reserves and bird watching centres should you want to get your binos out and see if you can spy the Ospreys that have since 1996 made the lake one of their breeding sites. There are many species of birds on the reservoir and the wildfowl in winter can exceed 20,000 in number.

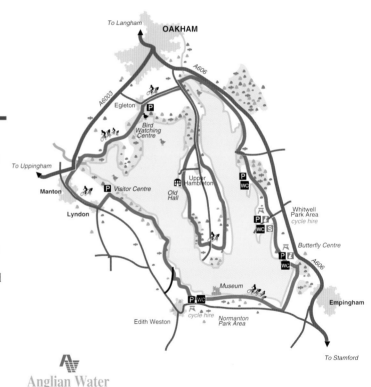